THE
ROYAL
FAMILY

THE
ROYAL
FAMILY

Gareth Thomas

Photographs by the

PaRragon

Bath · New York · Singapore · Hong Kong · Cologne · Delhi · Melbourne

First published by Parragon in 2007

Parragon
Queen Street House, 4 Queen Street, Bath, BA1 1HE, UK

Produced by Atlantic Publishing

Photographs © Associated Newspapers archive
Text © Parragon Books Ltd 2007

ISBN 978-1-4054-8809-9
Printed in China

Contents

THE ROYAL FAMILY

The origins of our Royal Family can be traced back to George III's reign in the 18th century, although it was not until 1917 that anti-German feeling led George V to discard the historic name of Saxe-Coburg-Gotha and adopt the family name of 'Windsor', applying it to the title of the Royal House.

The Windsors' reign over almost a century has seen monumental political and social change: from first flight to lunar landings; from universal suffrage to the election of a female Prime Minister; through two World Wars, the Cold War, more recent conflicts in the Middle East and the emergence of international terrorism; not to mention the birth of the 'talkies', television, a National Health Service, education as a right, the Swinging Sixties, the collapse of the Soviet system and the rise of the computer age.

The list goes on, as does the Royal Family, taking in its stride the many events that have shaped and transformed the country and the world over the past decades. It has had its own share of trials and tribulations – the abdication crisis of Edward VIII, the very public disclosures following the divorce of the Prince and Princess of Wales and the death of Diana in 1997 – but these have been counterbalanced by happier events such as the Silver Wedding Anniversary of the Queen and Duke of Edinburgh, the Queen's Silver Jubilee, culminating in the Queen's Golden Jubilee of 2002.

The media, and it might be said the public's, fascination with the Royals has grown to unprecedented levels over the last quarter of a century, and for the most part, remains undiminished. The House of Windsor has had to adapt to increasing press and public scrutiny during this time, and accept that the days of unquestioning reverence have passed. Despite the concern whether the British monarchy can sustain itself in its current form, the Royal Family remains deeply enshrined as an institution, providing for many a sense of enduring stability and order, and its contributions to our cultural and social history through charity work and official Royal engagements cannot be denied.

This book is a 'right royal' celebration of a truly remarkable family – a story told in pictures taken from the archives of the Daily Mail, many of which are seen here in print for the first time.

THE YOUNG PRINCES

Edward and Albert were the eldest of six children born to George V and Princess Mary. As the first-born, Edward was natural heir to the throne.

Opposite right: Edward, resplendent in naval uniform at Buckingham Palace in 1911, shortly after his father's coronation as King George V, and his own investiture as the Prince of Wales.

Below: Edward shooting at Balmoral later that same year. Meanwhile, his father was hunting tigers whilst on a state visit to India.

Opposite left: Even as a young man, the Prince was renowned for his attention to detail when it came to being properly dressed for any given occasion.

Above: Edward's younger brother, Prince Albert, the Duke of York, during his naval schooling, aged 16.

Right: A somewhat awkward and unacademic youth, Prince Albert led a rather unhappy childhood, no doubt partly on account of the social stigma associated with his left-handedness. However, he would later excel at sports, particularly tennis, although here he can be seen playing golf.

WARTIME DUTIES

Below: Having pursued a career in the Royal Navy from a relatively early age, King George V was no stranger to uniform and had risen to the rank of Commander by 1890. However at the outbreak of WWI in 1914, he feared for the safety of his son, Prince Albert, who would see action two years later at the Battle of Jutland. The King and Queen are pictured with the two princes, President and Madame Poincaré and Sir Douglas Haig.

Opposite above: King George himself performed numerous wartime duties, including visiting civilians both at home and abroad in an effort to boost morale. Here he greets French villagers.

Opposite below left: The King also made several visits to the troops in order to make inspections and to present thousands of bravery medals, even visiting the trenches of the Western Front on five occasions.

Opposite below right: King George meets with General Congreve and Sir Henry Rawlinson on a visit to the Western Front.

Prince Albert Marries

Opposite above: Prince Albert married Elizabeth Bowes-Lyon at Westminster Abbey on April 26th 1923. The two had first met as children and Prince Albert had long had his heart set on wooing Lady Elizabeth.

Right: The Duke and Duchess of York take a walk through the grounds of Polesden Lacey in Surrey during their honeymoon.

Above right: The couple relaxing during their Royal Honeymoon, after a game of golf. They spent the first few years of their marriage living in Bruton Street, London.

Above left: The Duke and Duchess of York with Queen Mary at Balmoral in 1924.

Opposite below: The Duke of York with various dignitaries, including the Vice-Chancellor, Chief Constable, Pro Vice-Chancellor and Lord Mayor, whilst on a visit to Leeds in 1925. Despite numerous public appearances, the Duke often struggled with public speaking because of a severe stammer.

THE INTER-WAR YEARS

Right: Edward, the Prince of Wales, attended by his train-bearer as he is installed as the Chancellor of the University of Wales in Cardiff.

Below: Queen Mary and Prince George visiting the British Empire Exhibition at Wembley in 1924, which had been officially opened by King George V.

Opposite top: King George V and Queen Mary at the Royal Pavilion, Aldershot, with the Secretary of State for War, the Right Honourable Stephen Walsh.

Opposite below: Prince Albert and Elizabeth, the Duke and Duchess of York, on a visit to Millwall docks in 1924. After WWI, Albert became President of the Industrial Welfare Society, and was actively involved in establishing programmes for helping young workers.

ELIZABETH AND MARGARET, THE YOUNG PRINCESSES

Left: During an outing to the cinema shortly after the birth of their first child, Elizabeth, on April 21st 1926, the Duke and Duchess of York were presented with a teddy bear by a well-wisher.

Below right: The young Princess Elizabeth on a drive from Buckingham Palace in 1927, accompanied by her nanny, Clare 'Allah' Knight.

Below left: The following year, the young Princess Elizabeth aged two, leaving her Piccadilly home for a drive with her nanny. On August 21st 1930 Elizabeth gave birth to her second daughter, Margaret Rose.

Opposite below: The Duke of York with his father, the King, at Balmoral, having welcomed King Boris of Bulgaria for a brief visit.

Opposite above: The Duke and Duchess of York were to embark on their first major state visit in 1927, visiting Fiji, Australia and New Zealand, where they were able to enjoy a spot of fly fishing.

THREE GENERATIONS

The two young princesses often accompanied their parents on official engagements.

Above: The Queen, the Princess Royal, and the Duchess of York, with Princess Elizabeth on their way down The Mall to watch the Trooping of the Colour at Horse Guards Parade.

Right: The Duchess of York attended the Abergeldie Castle Fete in 1933, with her two daughters, Princess Elizabeth, aged seven, and Princess Margaret Rose, aged three. A picture of Buckingham Palace is visible on the Duchess's handbag.

Opposite above: The Duchess of York accompanied the King and Queen as they visited Southampton to open the world's largest dry dock.

Opposite below right: Princess Elizabeth leaving Westminster Abbey with her grandparents, King George and Queen Mary.

Opposite below left: Wearing the uniform of the Irish Guards, the King took part in the Trooping of the Colour at Horse Guards Parade, on the occasion of his 70th birthday.

KING GEORGE V'S SILVER JUBILEE

Opposite below left: King George greeting one of his admirals aboard the royal yacht, in 1935, the year of the Silver Jubilee celebrations, which commemorated the 25th anniversary of his accession to the throne.

Opposite below right: The Duke and Duchess of York, with the Duke and Duchess of Kent and the two young Princesses, leaving St. Paul's Cathedral, following the King George V Silver Jubilee Celebration Service.

Opposite above: Crowds line the Victoria Embankment, London, to catch a glimpse of the King and Queen as they returned from St. Paul's.

Above: The Lord Mayor of London presented the King with the ceremonial sword that is the symbol of the City of London's independence during the Temple Bar Ceremony.

Left: The Duke and Duchess of York boarding an airliner at Hendon as they prepared to visit the International Exhibition in Brussels. Whilst this was to be the Duchess's first flight, the Duke had previously become the first royal to obtain a pilot's licence.

THE DEATH OF KING GEORGE V

Right: King George V died on January 20th 1936 and the following day the Prince of Wales was proclaimed King Edward VIII. Here he is pictured with the Duke of Kent, the Duke of York and the Duke of Gloucester on the eve of his coronation.

Below: The funeral of King George V took place on January 28th. A few days before, his body was brought from Sandringham to London, where the coffin was carried from the train at King's Cross.

Opposite above: The Princesses Elizabeth and Margaret with their parents, meeting members of the Royal Company of Archers.

Opposite below left: King Edward VIII delivered his first radio broadcast to his subjects from Broadcasting House in March 1936, shortly after being proclaimed king.

Opposite below right: The young princesses were already becoming involved in formal functions from a young age. Here they attended a tree-planting ceremony at Windsor Great Park.

A Royal Scandal

Opposite above: Within months of his accession to the throne, scandal erupted when the King's relationship with a married woman (Mrs Wallis Simpson) became common knowledge, and pressure mounted for him to abdicate. In December, 1936, Edward made his abdication speech from Windsor Castle before leaving the country to be with his lover in France, where they were married just six months later.

Opposite below: Wallis Simpson, lover of the former King Edward, becomes the Duchess of Windsor, as she marries the Duke in France.

Right: Although there were guests in attendance, members of the Royal Family were forbidden from attending the wedding by Edward's brother, the newly appointed King George VI.

Below: The Duke of Windsor and Mrs Simpson pose together for photographers at the Château de Cande.

RELUCTANT MONARCHS

After Edward's abdication the role of King fell to Albert who took the title of George VI to provide continuity for the troubled monarchy.

Opposite above: The Duke and Duchess of York became King and Queen, somewhat reluctantly leaving behind the promise of a quiet family life. Here they attended the State Opening of Parliament in May 1937, soon after their coronation.

Above: The King and Queen returning from a visit to Canada in 1939, accompanied by their daughters.

Opposite below right: Pictured in September 1939, the King had just made his broadcast to declare that Britain was at war with Germany.

Opposite below left: Two months later, the Queen broadcast to the nation, to reassure the mothers of evacuated children.

Left: The Princesses Elizabeth and Margaret at their war-time residence in Britain.

BRAVING THE BLITZ

Below: As a gesture of solidarity with the people of London, the King and Queen continued to reside at Buckingham Palace throughout the War, where they too were affected by the German bombing raids during the Blitz.

Right: The King and Queen surveying the damage to Buckingham Palace following an air raid on the night of September 13th 1940, which destroyed the chapel building.

Opposite above left: Accompanied by her husband and Prime Minister Churchill, the Queen spoke to workers who were helping to clear up after the bombing.

Opposite above right: Following the bombing, the Queen toured the East End of London, speaking to women and children who had also been affected.

Opposite below: Amid the debris from a bombed London hospital, the Queen paid tribute to the hospital workers, some of whom had been bombed out of their homes and yet continued to work long shifts on the wards.

THE ROYALS
DIG FOR VICTORY

Opposite above: As the war rumbled on, the British public increasingly took up the 'Dig for Victory' campaign, turning over large areas of land to cultivate crops to feed the populace. The Royal Family demonstrated their support, joining those harvesting crops grown at Sandringham.

Opposite below: In a bid to save fuel whilst inspecting the Sandringham House harvest, the King and Princesses travelled by bicycle, whilst the Queen made use of a pony and trap.

Above: Here the teenage Princesses can be seen gathering crops in August 1943.

Centre: The Sandringham farm workers and their families were entertained and rewarded with a garden party, at which the Royals mingled freely with their guests.

Left: The King and Queen met with the Sandringham farm manager, Mr. A. Mackinnon, and Captain C.A. Pelham-Welby.

Princess Elizabeth's Wedding

Above: Two years after the end of WWII, the Royal Family, and the nation, celebrated as Princess Elizabeth married Lieutenant Philip Mountbatten, nephew of Lord Mountbatten, on November 20th 1947. Although originally of Greek citizenship, Philip was able to convert to British citizenship due to the fact that he had fought for the United Kingdom, and he duly received the title Prince Philip, Duke of Edinburgh.

Left: Princess Elizabeth was escorted by the Household Cavalry to Westminster Abbey in the Irish State Coach.

Opposite: Princess Elizabeth and Prince Philip leaving Westminster Abbey after the wedding ceremony. They travelled to Lord Mountbatten's Romsey estate, Broadlands, to begin their honeymoon.

Welcome Prince Charles

Right: Princess Elizabeth gave birth to her first child, Charles Philip Arthur George, on November 14th 1948. Here they are pictured at his christening, which took place at Buckingham Palace on the 15th December.

Below right: A young Prince Charles taken for a walk by his nanny.

Below: Princess Margaret seen on the balcony of Buckingham Palace, following the Trooping of the Colour Ceremony.

Top: The King and Queen lead the Royal Family and other dignitaries into Buckingham Palace following a Royal Garden Party.

Above: The Princess Royal, Duke of Edinburgh, Princess Margaret, Lord Rosebery and the Duke of Gloucester enjoying a summer's day at the races at Epsom, Surrey.

Left: Later in the year, the King and Queen attend the wedding of Princess Elizabeth's Lady-in-Waiting, Lady Margaret Egerton and the Princess's private secretary, Mr. John Colville, in Westminster.

TIME IN SCOTLAND

Left: Whilst in Scotland the Royal Family, including the King and Queen, the Marquess of Aberdeen, the Duke and Duchess of Gloucester, the Duke of Edinburgh, Princess Margaret and Princess Elizabeth, attended the Braemar Games.

Centre: King George VI and Queen Elizabeth with Princess Elizabeth and the young Prince Charles, were greeted by the Provost of Ballater on arrival at Ballater Station en route to Balmoral Castle for a holiday in 1949.

Opposite above left: The King, Queen and Princess Margaret visit children at the Northern Infirmary in Inverness, Scotland.

Opposite above right: On return from Scotland Royal engagements continued. However with the King's health failing, Princess Elizabeth took her father's place during the Trooping of the Colour Ceremony in 1949, riding out on horseback at Horse Guards Parade.

Below: The King and Queen at the Royal Garden Party at Buckingham Palace.

Opposite below: The Queen and various members of the Royal Family on the balcony of Buckingham Palace for the Trooping of the Colour Ceremony in 1951. King Haakon of Norway was also in attendance.

QUEEN ELIZABETH II

Opposite: On the 6th February 1952, King George VI died in his sleep after a long struggle with illness. The nation mourned his loss, but prepared to welcome Princess Elizabeth as the new Queen, Elizabeth II. Here she takes the salute at the Trooping of the Colour Ceremony in June.

Left: The former Queen, having now become the Queen Mother, is pictured with Princess Margaret at the Trooping of the Colour.

Above left: Here Elizabeth is seen on her way to dinner at the French Embassy in London.

Above right: Elizabeth's daughter Anne was born on August 14th 1950. She attended her first public engagement following the birth at London's Royal College of Music.

THE YOUNG ROYAL FAMILY

Below: In September 1952, Queen Elizabeth II, and Prince Philip were joined at Balmoral Castle by King Feisal and the Regent of Iraq. Princess Anne was just over two years old.

Opposite above left: Elizabeth and Margaret attending the State Opening of Parliment.

Opposite above right: Elizabeth and Margaret playing with Princess Anne at Balmoral Castle the day after Margaret's 21st Birthday.

Opposite below: Queen Elizabeth and Prince Philip with their children, Charles and Anne, at their Clarence House home in London.

Left: A Garden Party at Buckingham Palace.

THE CORONATION OF QUEEN ELIZABETH II

Opposite above left: Elizabeth was officially crowned Queen on the 2nd June 1953 at Westminster Abbey, with some 8000 people in attendance, whilst millions more were able to watch the ceremony on television for the first time. Here she begins her journey to the Abbey in the Gold State Coach.

Opposite above right: Wearing a simple white dress, the Queen is seated in the St. Edward's Chair, surrounded by Knights of the Garter.

Right: Having spoken private prayers, the Queen took the Chair of Estate.

Opposite below left: Here she bears the Rod with Dove, symbol of equity and mercy in her left hand, and the Sceptre with Cross, the symbol of power and justice, in her right, whilst the Archbishop of Canterbury prepares to position the St. Edward's Crown on her head.

Below: Following the Coronation, the Queen and her attendants proceeded from Westminster Abbey.

Opposite below right: That evening, the Queen appeared on the balcony of Buckingham Palace to greet the adoring crowds that thronged below and to witness a flypast salute by the Royal Air Force.

A Queen and Mother

Opposite above: One year after the Queen's coronation, her official birthday is marked by an RAF flypast over Buckingham Palace. The Queen Mother, Prince Charles and Princess Anne were amongst those present on the balcony at Buckingham Palace to witness the event.

Above: The following year, as the Royal Family gathered to watch the Trooping of the Colour, the crowds chanted birthday wishes to the Duke of Edinburgh on the occasion of his 33rd birthday.

Opposite below left: The Queen pictured at Balmoral with Princess Anne and her pony Greensleeves during their summer holiday there in 1955.

Opposite below right: In November that year, Queen Elizabeth attended the annual Royal Variety Show at Victoria Palace Theatre.

Opposite centre right: The Queen arriving at Westminster Abbey, cloaked in white mink, for the Order of the Bath Ceremony in 1956.

Right: The Queen with Lord Mountbatten at the premiere of 'Dunkirk' in 1958. This was the same month in which the last debutantes would be presented before her at the Royal Court.

PRINCESS MARGARET MARRIES

Right: On May 6th 1960, Princess Margaret was married to photographer Antony Armstrong-Jones in a fairy-tale ceremony at Westminster Abbey. After the service, the happy couple, with a rose petal send-off, embarked on their honeymoon on the Royal Yacht, Britannia.

Opposite above: The young Princess Anne was amongst the eight bridesmaids, and can be seen here (left) beside the Queen and Queen Mother who wave goodbye from the Palace forecourt as the newlyweds leave for their honeymoon.

Below: On February 19th 1960, the Queen gave birth to her third child and second son, Andrew. Here she is pictured with her husband, three children, and one of her beloved corgis at Balmoral.

Opposite below: The Queen Mother holds the infant Prince Andrew on the occasion of her 60th birthday at Clarence House. Prince Charles and Princess Anne were also there to enjoy the celebrations.

THE PUBLIC FACE

Opposite below: In November 1958, the Queen attended a dinner held at the American Embassy in London, which was being hosted by the American Vice-President, Richard Nixon.

Left: Later in the year, she was present at the Odeon, Leicester Square for the première of Danny Kaye's film 'Me and the Colonel', where guests included Nicole Maurey and Mr and Mrs Kurt Jurgens.

Below: During the summer of 1959 the Queen visited the Royal Botanical Gardens at Kew, which celebrated its bicentenary. She visited the refurbished Palm House and took tea in the Orangery.

Opposite above: The Queen and Duke of Edinburgh relaxing in the grounds of Windsor Castle.

PRESENTATIONS AND WEDDINGS

Opposite above right: On her 35th Birthday in April 1961, the Queen attended the three-day horse trials at Badminton.

Opposite above left: In June of that year, the Queen met the new President of the United States of America, John F. Kennedy and his wife, Jackie, at a reception held at Buckingham Palace.

Below right: That same month, the Duke of Kent was married to Miss Katharine Worsley. He wore the uniform of his regiment, the Royal Scots Guards.

Opposite below left: Princess Margaret and her husband, Antony Armstrong-Jones, attending the Duke of Kent's wedding. Shortly afterwards, Armstrong-Jones was to accept the title, Earl of Snowdon.

Opposite below right: In July, the Queen presented the John Player trophy to Pat Smythe, the winner of the International Horse Show-Jumping Competition.

Left: The following year she presented the Championships Trophy to Rod Laver, winner of the Men's Singles Competition at Wimbledon.

Below left: In October 1962, the Queen greeted the stars at the Royal Command Performance held at the London Palladium. She can be seen shaking hands with Cliff Richard, who stands alongside Harry Secombe and Eartha Kitt.

PRINCE EDWARD

Opposite above and below: On March 10th 1964, the Queen gave birth to her fourth child, Prince Edward. The Queen and her family, including baby Edward, are pictured together at Frogmore, Windsor, on her 39th birthday.

Above left: The Queen attended the Gala performance of 'Tosca' in July 1965, at Covent Garden.

Centre: That same month, Elizabeth II became the first reigning monarch since 1671 to make an official visit to the Isle of Wight.

Above right: Later in the year, the Queen attended the Royal Albert Hall for the St. Celia Festival Royal Charity Concert.

Left: The Queen was introduced to the comedian Ken Dodd at the Royal Variety Performance held at the London Palladium. Dudley Moore, Spike Milligan and Max Bygraves are also pictured.

Royal Engagements

Opposite below right: At the end of 1968, the Queen, who had recently returned from a visit to South America, attended a service at St. George's Chapel, Windsor, with Princess Anne. They were met by the Dean of Windsor, the Very Reverend John Woods. Later, to mark the 50th anniversary of the Royal Air Force, the Queen was presented with a pair of large silver candlesticks.

Opposite above: The Queen met Joan Collins and William Dix at the première of 'Doctor Doolittle', at the Odeon, Leicester Square.

Above: In February 1969, The Queen and Prince Philip were joined for lunch at Buckingham Palace by the President of the United States, Richard Nixon.

Left: The following month, on the 7th March, the Queen officially opened the new Victoria Line of the London Underground, and became the first reigning monarch to make a journey on the system.

Opposite below left: The Royal Family pictured at Windsor, on the occasion of the Queen's 42nd birthday in 1968.

INVESTITURE OF PRINCE CHARLES

Right: 1969 was perhaps more significant and daunting for Prince Charles than for any other member of the Royal Family, as it was to be the year of his investiture as the Prince of Wales, a fact that was met with considerable resistance by Welsh Nationalists, who saw the ceremony as an act of English oppression. In an attempt to diffuse hostile opinion, the Prince spent a term at the University of Aberystwyth and a series of photos were published to show him in a more informal light. However on July 1st, the morning of the ceremony itself, two men were killed as they attempted to plant a bomb near Caernarvon Castle.

Opposite above: Prince Charles is seen leaving a church service with the Queen Mother and other members of the Royal Family.

Above right: Shortly after his investiture, the Prince conversed with guests at the Royal Garden Party at Buckingham Palace.

Opposite below: Prince Charles accompanied his parents and sister to the 25th anniversary Variety Performance, held in aid of the Army Benevolent Fund.

Above left: The Queen and Prince Philip are greeted by the Prime Minister, Harold Wilson, as they arrive for a ceremony to commemorate the 20th anniversary of the Signature of Statute of the Council of Europe.

FAMILY CELEBRATIONS

Above left: The Queen Mother celebrated her 70th birthday at Clarence House on the 4th August 1970, with Prince Edward and his young cousins, Lady Sarah and Viscount Linley.

Above right: The Queen and Prince Edward at Badminton in April 1971. The following year, Princess Anne went on to become European Champion at the three-day horse trials held at Burghleigh in September, despite an operation to remove an ovarian cyst the month before.

Right: Princess Anne and other members of the family coming ashore in Thurso from the Royal Yacht Britannia on the 15th August 1971, Anne's 21st birthday. Despite her youth, Anne had by now become President of the Save the Children Fund.

Opposite above: The Royal Family leaving St. George's Chapel, Windsor, on Christmas Day, 1971.

Opposite below: Here the Queen is seen attending the 'Treasures of Tutankhamun' exhibition in London in 1972.

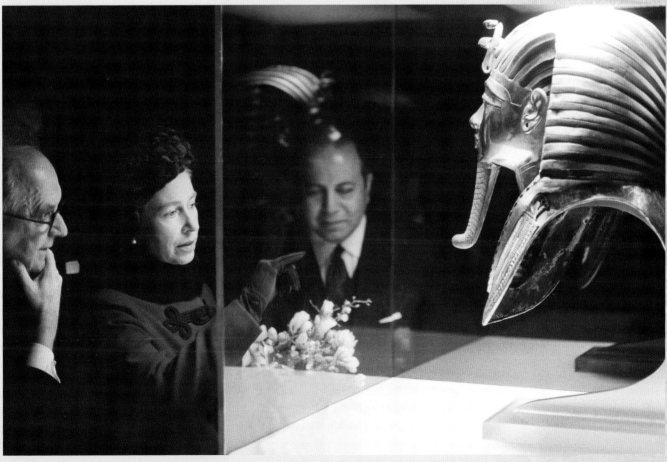

Silver Wedding Anniversary

Above: The year 1972 marked Queen Elizabeth II and Prince Philip's silver wedding anniversary. A series of photographs were commissioned to celebrate the event. Here the Royal Couple are pictured in the grounds of Balmoral.

Opposite below left: The Queen at Balmoral in 1972.

Opposite above: That same year also marked the centenary celebrations of St. Peter's Church of England School in London, which were attended by the Queen.

Left: Politically and economically, 1972 was important as the year in which Britain entered the Common Market. In January the following year, the Queen and Prince Philip attended the official 'Fanfare for Europe' Gala at Covent Garden to celebrate the event. The Queen is pictured with Edward Heath, the Prime Minister.

Opposite below right: The Queen visits the Boys' and Girls' Brigade Headquarters in London in February 1973.

Princess Anne Marries

Left: Princess Anne married Lieutenant Mark Phillips at Westminster Abbey on November 14th 1973. After the ceremony they greeted well-wishers from the balcony at Buckingham Palace.

Below left: Later that year the Queen visits Aberfan Cemetery in Wales, to lay a wreath at the slate memorial cross, which commemorates the loss of the 116 children and 28 adults who perished in 1966 in the Aberfan disaster. The village school was buried beneath thousands of tons of coal-waste that collapsed and slid from the hill above.

Below right: The Queen on her 48th Birthday in 1974 at Windsor, where she was to review the Queen's Scouts.

Opposite below: In March 1973, Eric Morecambe and Ernie Wise met the Queen at the Odeon Leicester Square, where they were attending the preview of 'Lost Horizon', starring Sir John Gielgud, Sally Kellerman and Peter Finch.

Opposite above: The Queen, Prince Philip and the young Royals visit the Duke of Beaufort's hounds.

STATE DUTIES

Left: The Queen pictured with Her Majesty's bodyguard of the Yeoman of the Guard, following an inspection at Buckingham Palace.

Opposite above right: The Queen attending the Royal Windsor Horse Show with King Constantine of Greece and the husband of Princess Margaretha of Sweden, Mr John Ambler, in July 1974.

Opposite below: The Queen visits the Chelsea Flower Show.

Below left: In July 1975, the Queen is introduced to the English cricket team by Captain Tony Greig, as they prepare to take on Australia in the 2nd Test.

Opposite above left: On his 26th birthday in November, Prince Charles went to see a production of Alan Ayckbourn's 'Third Person Singular' at the Vaudeville Theatre, accompanied by his mother and Princess Alexandra.

Below right: The following month, the Queen attended the film première of 'Rooster Cogburn' at the Odeon, Leicester Square. The event was held in aid of the Police Dependants' Trust, and Laura Gisbourne, the daughter of Police Inspector David Gisbourne who had died in the Red Lion riots the previous year, presented the Queen with a bouquet.

THE QUEEN'S SILVER JUBILEE, 1977

Opposite above: In 1977, both Queen and country celebrated 25 years of Elizabeth II's reign, and the public demonstrated massive support for the reigning monarch. She undertook an extensive tour of both the United Kingdom and the Commonwealth, during which huge crowds lined the streets and gathered outside Buckingham Palace to show their affection.

Opposite below right: The official celebrations began at Windsor in June, with the Queen lighting the first of 100 beacons, and with the Royal Family attending a special service at St. Paul's Cathedral.

Opposite below left: The Queen, Prince Philip and Prince Charles at St. Paul's.

Below right: Adoring crowds turned out to see the Queen on her visit to Brighton.

Left: Similar scenes were repeated during her visit to the Channel Islands in 1978.

Below left: In 1979, the Royal Family celebrated the Queen and Prince Philip's 32nd wedding anniversary at Balmoral.

CHARLES AND DIANA

Opposite above left: Although they had first met in 1977, it was not until 1980 that a relationship began to blossom between Prince Charles and Lady Diana Spencer, and the media began to take an increasing interest. When she returned home after a holiday at Balmoral with the Royal Family, she was to find the press camped outside her London flat.

Opposite above right: Diana worked as a kindergarten supervisor, and although not formally trained, demonstrated a natural ability when it came to caring for children.

Below: The relationship developed swiftly, and on February 24th 1981, the couple officially announced their engagement.

Left: Diana's engagement ring consisted of a large sapphire set in white gold, surrounded by 14 diamonds.

Opposite below: Diana soon moved in to Buckingham Palace and began to accompany the Prince on official functions and public events. Here she is pictured with Andrew Parker-Bowles at the Horse and Hound Grand Military Gold Cup at Sandown, in which Charles was competing.

THE ROYAL WEDDING

Opposite below: Charles and Diana's wedding was a truly spectacular occasion. The service took place at St. Paul's Cathedral, rather than at Westminster Abbey, as was more traditional, and the day was declared a public holiday. A million people were estimated to have lined the processional route from St. Paul's to Buckingham Palace, whilst some 700 million watched the proceedings on television.

Opposite above left: The newlyweds emerged from the Cathedral to rapturous applause, before proceeding to their waiting coach. Diana's dress had been made by Mrs Nina Missetzis, and included a 25-foot train.

Opposite above right: Accompanied by a mounted escort, the happy couple were conveyed to Buckingham Palace in their open-topped coach, where a huge crowd gathered to greet them for their appearance on the balcony.

Below right: A smiling Diana waves to the crowd.

Left: Charles and Diana on their honeymoon at Balmoral, following a brief stay at Broadlands, and a two week cruise around the Mediterranean aboard the Royal Yacht Britannia.

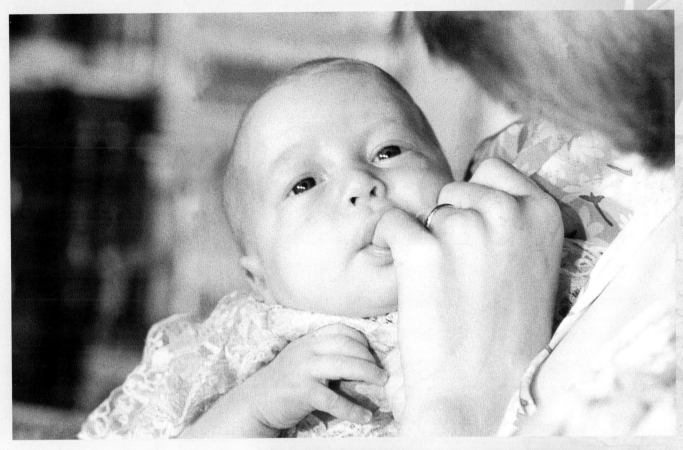

THE YOUNG PRINCES

Opposite below left: On June 21st 1982, just ten days before her 21st Birthday, Diana gave birth to her first child, Prince William, at the private wing of St. Mary's Hospital, London. Charles was present throughout the birth, and they left the hospital at 6pm the following day.

Opposite above: On the 4th August, the infant was christened William Arthur Philip Louis, at Buckingham Palace, putting an end to public and media speculation.

Above: The tiny Prince William held tightly in his mother's arms at the christening.

Right: Two years later, on September 15th 1984, the Princess gave birth to her second son, Prince Henry Charles Albert David.

Opposite below right: Hordes of photographers and well-wishers waited outside the hospital for the Princess to emerge with her newborn son.

PUBLIC ENGAGEMENTS

Above: Charles and Diana on a visit to Aberdovey in Wales, shortly after William's birth.

Centre: In June 1983, the Queen opened the new gardens at Croydon Town Hall, marking the centenary of the town's municipal charter.

Below: In June 1984, the Queen hosted a special banquet at Buckingham Palace following the London Economic Summit. Among the guests were the US President Ronald Reagan and British Premier Margaret Thatcher.

THE DUKE AND DUCHESS OF YORK

Left: Prince Andrew and Sarah Ferguson announced their engagement on March 19th 1986.

Below: They married four months later at Westminster Abbey on July 23rd After their marriage they were given the titles of Duke and Duchess of York.

PRINCESS OF WALES

Right: Princess Diana was an incredibly active and popular member of the Royal Family. Here she greets the crowds as she visits St. Catherine's Hospice in Crawley, Surrey, in 1988.

Opposite above: Princess Diana and Princess Michael are pictured with their children watching the Trooping of the Colour parade in June.

Opposite below: In March 1988, the Queen and Prince Philip attended the Maundy Service at Lichfield Cathedral, where members of the local community received the Maundy Money.

Below right: Here, Her Majesty is pictured with the Right Reverend Keith Sutton, Lord Bishop of Lichfield.

Below left: The Queen planting the 'Chelsea Sentinel' in the grounds of the Royal Hospital, Chelsea.

School Days

Opposite above right: William began his final year at Wetherby pre-prep school by attending the Harvest Festival at St. Matthew's Church, Bayswater.

Opposite above left: William playing football for Wetherby School in their first match of the season against Bassett House of Kensington.

Left: William was met by headmaster Gerald Barber as he began his first day at boarding school in September 1990, attending Ludgrove Preparatory School in Berkshire.

Opposite below right: Harry walking in the school crocodile with classmates to the annual school carol service.

Opposite below left: A right royal tantrum for Princess Beatrice.

PRINCESS ANNE REMARRIES

Left: Princess Anne at Charter House College of Radiography two days before her wedding.

Left below: Princess Anne and Commander Timothy Laurence were married on December 12th 1992. She chose the Church of Scotland as the Church of England forbade divorcees from remarrying. This photograph shows them leaving Crathie Church near Balmoral Castle.

Opposite above right: Harry's sixth birthday treat was a visit to the Battle of Britain 50th anniversary exhibition with a group of school friends.

Opposite above left: William finding his feet on a skiing holiday in Austria.

Opposite below left: The Duchess of York and her daughters, Princess Beatrice and Princess Eugenie.

Opposite below right: With everyone else posing for pictures at the wedding of Annabella Palumbo, Bridesmaid Princess Beatrice is more interested in her own royal walkabout.

DIFFICULT DAYS

Charles and Diana's relationship was now under great strain.

Opposite left: Princess Diana sits before the Taj Mahal and perhaps pauses for a moment of reflection whilst on a visit to India in 1992.

Left and below: William began his schooling at Eton in September 1995. Although by this time his parents were in the process of divorcing, the family arrived together.

Opposite below right and centre: The marriage of the Duke and Duchess of York was finally dissolved in 1996.

Opposite above right: Thorpe Park proved a firm favourite with Princes William and Harry, who returned to enjoy a day out there with their mother.

THE DEATH OF THE PRINCESS

Opposite above left: In 1995, Princess Diana had been awarded the Humanitarian of the Year Award, in recognition of the compassionate work she had undertaken for over 15 years. This continued in 1997 with a campaign against landmines, which saw her travelling to Angola on behalf of the Red Cross and the Halo Trust.

Left: On the 31st August 1997, Princess Diana was tragically killed in a high-speed car crash in Paris. The Princes, who were with their father at Balmoral at the time were informed the following morning. Immediately the announcement was made public, a massive outpouring of grief seemed to sweep the nation, with floral tributes swamping the entrance to Kensington Palace.

Below: Diana's funeral took place at Westminster Abbey on September 6th. One million people were estimated to have lined the procession route.

Opposite above right: Prince Charles attempts to console his distraught sons.

Opposite below: Charles, Prince Philip, the young Princes and Earl Spencer, Diana's brother, stand in silence as the coffin is carried past them into the Abbey.

EDWARD AND SOPHIE

Below: Prince Edward married Sophie Rhys-Jones on June 19th 1999. Breaking with tradition they chose to have the service at St. George's Chapel, Windsor. Afterwards, Edward was given the title Earl of Wessex and Sophie became HRH The Countess of Wessex.

Opposite below: The Princes joking with their father following William's first driving lesson at Highgrove in July 1999. His lesson had been given by police driving instructor, Sergeant Chris Gilbert.

Opposite above: In the years following the death of Princess Diana, the Princes perhaps naturally appeared to develop a closer bond with their father. Here they enjoy a skiing holiday at Klosters in Switzerland.

Left: On March 30th 2002, the Queen Mother died at the age of 101 after a long period of ill health. The Princes, her great-grandsons, followed the gun carriage that carried her coffin to Westminster, where she would lie-in-state until her funeral on April 9th.

GOLDEN JUBILEE

Opposite above left: In June 2002, Queen Elizabeth II celebrated her Golden Jubilee, having reigned as monarch for 50 years. The event was marked by extensive celebrations, including a thanksgiving service at St.Paul's Cathedral, a parade and carnival along The Mall, a flypast involving the Red Arrows and Concorde, the Party at the Palace concert at Buckingham Palace, and a huge firework display. Here the Queen makes her way to St. Paul's in the Gold State Coach, which she had previously used only for her coronation and Silver Jubilee celebrations.

Opposite above right: Edward and Sophie, the Earl and Countess of Wessex, leave Buckingham Palace for St.Paul's in an open-topped coach.

Left: Andrew, the Duke of York, and Princes William and Harry also ride in an open carriage as part of the procession, accompanied by a mounted escort.

Below: The Princes arriving at St. Paul's.

Opposite below: Prince William, Prince Charles and the Queen sharing a joke as they observe the spectacular carnival in The Mall.

CHARLES AND CAMILLA

Left: On April 9th 2005, Prince Charles married Camilla Parker-Bowles, who then became the Duchess of Cornwall. The ceremony took place at the Guildhall in Windsor.

Below: Pictured are Prince William, Prince Harry, and Peter and Zara Phillips, following the marriage blessings at St. George's Chapel, Windsor.

Opposite above left: In July, Prince Charles visited the site of a more recent conflict, the Old Bridge in Mostar, Bosnia, which had recently been rebuilt.

Opposite below: That same month, Prince Charles and his sons attended the official opening of the Diana Memorial Fountain in Hyde Park, London.

Opposite above right: On a somewhat happier note, July also saw the Party in the Park at Hyde Park, in aid of the Prince's Trust. Prince Charles is pictured with the singer Jamelia who is an ambassador for the organisation.

WILLIAM GRADUATES

Left: In June 2005 Prince William graduated from university, having gained a Masters Degree in Geography from the University of St. Andrews, Scotland.

Below: In the same month, the Prince and his wife arrive in the Royal Carriage for Ladies' Day at the Royal Ascot race meeting. The event was held at York on account of construction work being undertaken at Ascot Racecourse.

Opposite right: The Duchess of Cornwall, is pictured with Prince Charles, opening a playground near Balmoral; her first official engagement since they were married.

Opposite left: The Queen and Prince Philip attend The Order of the Garter Ceremony at Windsor Castle in full regalia.

A QUEEN AND HER HEIR

Her Majesty Queen Elizabeth II and Prince Charles attend Westminster Abbey in traditional red and white robes for the Most Honourable Order of the Bath Ceremony in May 2006. The ceremony dates back to medieval times and involves the installation of new knights into the chivalric order.

Acknowledgements

The photographs in this book are from the archives of the Daily Mail.
Particular thanks to Steve Torrington, Dave Sheppard, Brian Jackson,
Alan Pinnock, Katie Lee, Richard Jones and all the staff.

Thanks also to Alison Gauntlett, Sarah Rickayzen.
Design by John Dunne.